CW01651180

FOLLOWERS

Written by Pia Ashberry
Illustrated by Aafke Brouwer

Collins Educational
An imprint of HarperCollins*Publishers*

Chapter One

•••••••

Not Really Following

Rajinder saw it first. She'd gone to buy some milk for her mum, and there it was, as clear as anything. She said she'd stared at it for a minute, and then ran all the way back to our block to tell me. The first I knew about it was hearing a loud banging on our door. Mum opened it.

"Where's the fire?" she asked, as I looked past at Rajinder, who was desperately trying to catch her breath.

"Lisa... you've got to... it's..."

"What's the matter, Jin?" I asked, moving towards the door.

"You've got to come with me!"

"Is something wrong?" Mum asked, sounding worried.

"No, nothing," said Rajinder. "I just want to show Lisa something."

"Don't be long then," said Mum. "You haven't even had your breakfast."

Rajinder practically pulled me out of the door.

"Come on!" she shouted, as she ran towards the stairwell.

Carter's Newsagent
Premises to Rent
Fish

"What is it? Jin, just tell me what it is!"

Rajinder ignored my pleas, and kept on running. I gave up, and concentrated on keeping up with her. We reached the bottom of the stairs, and even then she didn't stop. She tore across the estate, past all the other tower blocks, and across the square of grass, with the funny-shaped statue. As we turned the corner, onto the parade of shops, I saw it. I stopped running and we linked arms, walking slowly towards it. And as we stood in front of it, Rajinder just turned to me and grinned.

"We did it, Lisa, we did it."

I grinned back proudly, and gazed at what used to be Mr Carter's newsagent's. The windows and door were boarded up and there was a 'PREMISES TO RENT' sign in the front.

We had worked hard to see that sign up there. We had worked all summer. I thought about how it had all begun – on the first day of the holidays...

That morning, I had woken up early, feeling great. Six weeks of freedom. Unbelievable.

"What are you going to do today?" asked Mum.

"Don't know, yet," I said. "Go round to Rajinder's first."

"Make sure you stay on the estate. I don't want you wandering off all over."

"I won't."

"Won't what? Stay on the estate or wander off?" she asked.

"I will."

"You will stay on the estate, or you will wander off?" said Mum, laughing.

"I will stay on the estate and I won't wander off," I promised.

My friend Rajinder lives on the second floor and we live on the eighth. The lift was broken, so I used the stairs. I rang Rajinder's bell, and waited.

Nothing happened for ages. I rang the bell again. Still nothing. I shouted, "Rajinder! It's me! It's Lisa!"

Mr Singh opened the door.

"Sorry, Lisa. Rajinder can't come out today. She's got too much homework."

"But Mr Singh, it's the holidays."

"What? Oh yes. Well, she has too much to do. Sorry."

He shut the door.

It was strange. He and Rajinder's mum always invited me in, even if they were busy. But this time it seemed he couldn't wait to get rid of me. I could hear Rajinder and her mum and dad inside talking in Punjabi. They were talking loudly, maybe even arguing, but I couldn't really tell. Suddenly, the door opened. It was Rajinder.

"Come on," she said. "Let's go."

"But your dad..."

"It's OK. He's said I could come out," she said. She kicked the wall as she spoke.

"He seemed upset."

"He's fine."

I thought they'd probably had an argument, but Rajinder didn't seem to want to talk about it, so I dropped it. We walked down the stairs and sat on the wall outside our block of flats.

"What are we going to do then?" I asked.

"Following. Let's do some following," said Rajinder.

"You're joking," I grinned. "You know we can't."

Following was a sort of game Rajinder and I used to play. You pick a person walking by and make up who they are and where they're going. Then you follow them to see if you're right.

We used to play it a lot, until we scared a woman from the first floor by following her to the shops. She thought we were going to mug her, but then she recognised us and complained to our parents.

My mum had been really angry. I tried to explain that we didn't follow anyone very far, and we never followed anyone who looked dangerous. It didn't help. I had promised not to play it again.

"We could just play it on the estate," said Rajinder.

"We said we wouldn't," I reminded her.

"All right. We needn't follow anyone then. We could just kind of watch them instead."

I thought for a moment. Mum couldn't stop us *watching* people. She did it to the neighbours all the time.

"OK," I said. "You go first."

Rajinder picked a woman coming out of the block opposite.

"Who is she then?" I asked as we watched her walk towards us.

"A famous film star," said Rajinder.

"Why's she living on this estate then?" I asked.

"Because she's fed up with being recognised and asked for autographs all the time. She just wants to live a quiet life, with her faithful dog for company," explained Rajinder.

Carter's Newsagent

"What's her dog's name then?"

"Fido," said Rajinder, trying to keep a straight face.

"Where's she going?"

"To meet the director of her new film."

The woman stopped in front of the post box. She took a letter from her bag, posted it, and turned back towards her block.

"What are you two gawping at?" she said as she passed by us.

"Can we have your autograph please?" Rajinder shouted after her, and we cracked up, laughing.

Chapter Two

Carter's, The Newsagent's

Later that morning, I spotted Mrs Blake from the seventh floor of our block, heading towards the shops.

"Who's that suspicious-looking character?" I asked.

"That's Betty Blake," giggled Rajinder. "Master criminal, responsible for thousands of unsolved crimes."

"She looks like she's going shopping to me."

"That's just a very clever disguise," said Rajinder.

"She always goes on a job with her shopping bag. It's her trademark. Bag lady Blake, they call her."

"Is she on a job now, then?" I asked.

"Yes. She's going to hold up Mr Carter, in the newsagent's."

"What, with a gun?"

"No," said Rajinder. "With her umbrella. She'll hit him over the head with it, and then fill up her bag with sweets, crisps and packets of cigarettes. She smokes like a chimney."

We ran after Mrs Blake and sure enough, when she reached the row of shops, it was the newsagent's that she went into. We waited for a few minutes and then followed her in.

She was nowhere to be seen.

"Excuse me," I said to Mr Carter. "Where's Mrs Blake?"

"Who?"

"The woman who just came in here."

"I don't know what you're talking about," he said.

"You must have seen her," said Rajinder.

"Did she go into the back?" I asked, pointing to a door at the far end of the shop.

"What is this? The third degree? Mind your own business," he snapped.

"We only want to know where she went," I said.

"Nobody's come in here, except you two. Now if you aren't going to buy anything, clear off. I've got better things to do than stand here talking to a couple of nosy kids. Go on, get lost."

"Horrible man," said Rajinder, when we got outside.

"Where is she?" I asked. "We saw her go in there."

"Don't know. Maybe she's made herself invisible. Or maybe she's an alien from another planet," Rajinder grinned.

"I'm being serious. She must have gone into the back," I said.

"Then why didn't he tell us? It's not as if it's against the law," argued Rajinder.

"Maybe they're both up to something," I said. "Come on, let's have a look round the back."

We went round the corner to the back of the row of shops. There were two windows at the back of the newsagents.

"She must be in there," I said.

"Yes, having a cup of tea, with Mrs Carter," said Rajinder.

I could tell she was getting bored.

"Come on Rajinder, don't spoil it."

"OK, let's find out," said Rajinder, and marched straight up to the window on the left. I hung back a little, to check there was no-one around.

"There's nobody in there," said Rajinder. "It's a lounge, but she isn't in it. Your turn now. Go and look through the other window."

I hesitated, and then walked slowly towards the other window. I crouched beneath it.

"Go on," said Rajinder. "Look!"

I raised my head to the level of the window, and immediately ducked down again.

"She's in there," I said. "With Mr Carter."

"Yes, sure," said Rajinder.

"She is. Come and look."

Rajinder came over and together we looked into a storeroom piled high with rows and rows of boxes. The newsagent and Mrs Blake were standing in one of the middle of these rows talking.

"Who's minding the shop?" asked Rajinder.

"Go and see. I'll wait here."

Rajinder ran off, but was back only a few seconds later.

"It's closed," she said when she reached me. "He's closed the shop. It's very strange..."

"They must be up to something," I said.

Once more, we looked through the window. Mr Carter and Mrs Blake were bending over a large box. He was holding a small knife.

"He's going to murder her!" I whispered.

"Don't be stupid. He's just going to open the box," hissed Rajinder.

"What do you think is in there? Car radios or videos?"

"More like five dozen packets of cheese and onion crisps," giggled Rajinder.

"Ssssh. They'll hear you."

The newsagent had now cut through the tape binding the box. I could tell that Rajinder, standing beside me, was holding her breath.

We watched as Mr Carter's hand reached down into the box and came back up with the contents.

Chapter Three

Taking A Risk

"Leaflets," I moaned, filled with disappointment. "It's just a load of boring old leaflets. Come on, let's go."

"Wait a minute," said Rajinder.

She was still staring into the storeroom.

"What for? Let's go. I'm hungry." I walked away from the window, but Rajinder stayed where she was.

"I want to know what those leaflets say," she whispered.

"They're probably for some stupid free pizza delivery or something," I said.

"I don't think so," Rajinder shook her head.

"What are you on about?" I realised she looked worried – even a little frightened.

"They look like..." Rajinder began, and then stopped.

"What? What do they look like?" I asked.

"Nothing." She shook her head.

"Jin, if you've got something to say, just say it."

"I haven't."

"You big liar," I said.

"Lisa, why don't you go and get your lunch? I'll see you tomorrow."

"I'm not going anywhere until you tell me what's going on."

Rajinder moved away from the window.

"We've been getting leaflets through the door, 'PAKIS GO HOME' and that sort of thing. Some of it is really nasty. This might be where they're coming from."

"Why didn't you tell me?"

"What's the point? What could you do?"

"I don't know. Something."

I remembered the strange look on Mr Singh's face, when he'd opened the door that morning.

"Is that why your dad didn't want you to come out?" I said.

"Yes. He worries about me."

We went back to Rajinder's for lunch, but we didn't say anything to her dad. Rajinder didn't want to upset him. Both of us were quiet, thinking about the leaflets.

After lunch we went to the playground and sat on the swings.

"I'm going back to the newsagent's," said Rajinder, breaking the silence. "Are you coming?"

"What for?"

"To see what those leaflets are, of course," she said. "To see if they really are what I think they are."

"Jin, you can't," I said. "It's dangerous. That man's horrible."

"Lisa," said Rajinder, very quietly. "I'm going over there, and I'm going now. So you can come with me or you can stay here. Either way, I'm still going."

And she began to walk away.

"I'll come with you," I said. "Of course I'll come with you."

Well, I couldn't let her do whatever she was going to do alone.

We walked slowly to the newsagent's, with Rajinder telling me her plan as we went. She was going to stand near the storeroom door and pretend to look at something. I was going to ask for something which I knew was kept behind the counter.

When the newsagent turned his back, Rajinder would nip though the door, find the leaflets, take a handful and escape through the window.

To start with, everything went well.

Mr Carter was stacking cigarettes when we went in. He looked around and then went on stacking. Rajinder had plenty of time to go into the storeroom.

"A packet of red balloons, please," I said.

The newsagent reached for a packet.

"Where's that Paki friend of yours?" he asked, as he handed me the balloons. "I saw two of you come in here."

"She's gone outside. And she isn't a Paki. She isn't even from Pakistan. She was born here, and so was her mum, and her dad was born in India."

"I don't give a monkey's where she was born. And give me those balloons back. I don't sell things to cheeky kids. You can go elsewhere in future. You're banned."
Mr Carter stared straight at me, as if he hated me.

"Suits me," I said, dropping the balloons. "I don't buy from racists anyway."

I ran out of the shop. My chest felt tight, the way it does when you have an argument.

I knew I had made him angry, but I didn't care. I took a deep breath and went round the back. I looked through the window. At first, I couldn't see Rajinder.

I stuck my face right up to the glass and, just as I did so, she appeared from behind a stack of boxes and came towards the window. She mouthed something at me that I couldn't understand. I shook my head.

She began to mime not being able to find the right box and I quickly pointed to where I thought the box had been. I watched as Rajinder searched box after box, finding nothing. Then, just as I started thinking that the box had been moved, she waved a stack of leaflets at me.

She started to read one. I couldn't believe it! Why was she wasting time like that?

After what seemed like ages she looked over at me and stuck her thumb up. She started moving towards the window, and then all of a sudden she froze. A cold shiver went down my spine.

"What's the matter?" I mouthed.

Jin gestured with her head to the right.

I looked, but I could see nothing. I could guess what was happening though. Mr Carter must be coming into the storeroom. He must have heard her. What would he do if he found Jin with the leaflets? Why had I agreed to this? I should have stopped her.

It was too late now.

Chapter Four

Caught!

"Hide!" I mouthed to Rajinder, who looked as if she had been turned to stone. The newsagent was in the room now – I could see him moving among the boxes. Rajinder hid behind a cupboard. I bobbed down.

I stayed frozen, my body pressed tight against the wall until I couldn't bear it any longer. I had to do something. But what? Go and tell Mr Singh? Call the police? Try and get into the storeroom myself?

But my legs refused to do anything.

I just sat there, unable to move.

"What do you think you're doing?"

I turned slowly to face the voice.

It was Mrs Blake!

"Nothing," I said, getting to my feet.

"Don't give me that," she said, taking hold of my shoulders. "I wasn't born yesterday. What are you up to?"

"I told you. Nothing. Just playing."

"All right. Have it your way. I'm sure Mr Carter will be able to get more out of you. He'll be very interested to know why you've been nosing round the back of his shop."

She took me by the arm and started to drag me along.

"No, please. I wasn't doing anything. Really I wasn't." I wriggled as hard as I could, trying to get away.

Mrs Blake took no notice. The more I struggled, the harder she held on to me.

"Let go. You're hurting me."

"Shut it," she said, and tightened her grip.

I looked back, but there was no sign of Jin. I was terrified she might think that I'd chickened out and left her.

That is, if she was still in the storeroom. For all I knew, she had been caught, too.

"Get in there, you little snooper."

Mrs Blake had opened the door and was trying to push me into the shop. I made a last, desperate attempt to get away, stamping on her foot as hard as I could.

Then, as she shrieked and loosened her grip, I kicked her and slipped out of her grasp.

"Oooh, you little... I'll get you for this," she shouted after me. "I know where you live."

I ran round the corner. Rajinder was there – halfway through the window.

"Hurry up," I shouted.

"What's the matter?"

"I'll tell you later," I said, grabbing her hand and yanking her to the ground. I knew Mrs Blake would be after us any second. I started to run, pulling Rajinder along with me. We didn't stop until we reached the playground where we collapsed onto the ground, panting.

Carter's Newsagent
the Paper

Neither Mrs Blake nor the newsagent were anywhere in sight.

"Imagine if she'd managed to get you into the shop," said Rajinder, after I'd told her what had happened.

"Or if he'd caught you in the storeroom," I said.

"Don't," she shuddered. " I don't even want to think about it."

"What about the leaflets?" I asked.

"They're the same ones all right," said Rajinder handing me one to read.

"So what do we do now?" I asked.

"I'm not sure. We can't go to the police. We'd get into trouble for breaking in there."

"How about the neighbourhood centre?"

The neighbourhood centre's on the estate. It's where you go to tell the council if you've got problems.

We decided to give it a try.

"We've had complaints about him before," said the woman there. "But he isn't a council tenant, I'm afraid. That means there's nothing we can do. You should really go to the police, and tell them about it."

I groaned.

"Do keep us informed though if anything else happens," the woman added.

"We can't go to the police," I sighed, as we left the building.

"No," said Rajinder. "But there is something we can do."

"What?" I asked.

"Well, you know he said he'd banned you."

"So?"

"We could do the same to him. Ban him."

"But it's his shop. How can we ban him from his own shop?"

"No, stupid," she said. "I mean ban his shop. Get people to stop using it."

"Jin, that's brilliant. We can get all our friends to ban it, and stand outside the shop with banners and things. Do you get it? Banners... to ban it... banners."

"Yes, Lisa, I get it. But we can't do that. It's too dangerous."

"What do you mean?" I asked.

"They don't just put leaflets through the letterbox you know."

I was silent for a moment. Until now I hadn't realised what a huge risk Rajinder had taken.

"But how will he know that he's banned?" I asked.

"*He* won't, but *we* will. And so will anyone else who joins in."

"OK," I said. "Let's start with everyone we know."

Chapter Five

The Ban

Over the next few weeks, we called round to see everyone we knew on the estate. Rajinder said it was too dangerous to call on people we didn't know – they might be racists like Mr Carter, or good friends of his and Mrs Blake. But we did tell all the black and Asian families. Most of them had been getting leaflets too, and were really relieved to find out who had sent them.

A lot of people said they would use the newsagent's shop on the main road instead, even though it was further away.

Mr and Mrs Waterfield from next door said that they had never liked Mr Carter anyway. Mr Waterfield said he was a miserable so-and-so.

All our friends joined in and promised to get the people they knew to ban him, too.

"Boycott, you mean," said Mum later when I was telling her about it. "You're boycotting him."

"What does that mean?" I asked.

Mum hesitated. "Same as ban really," she said finally.

We told Mum and Rajinder's parents about finding the leaflets in the back of the shop. Mr Singh went mad about Rajinder putting herself in danger, but you could tell he was proud of her as well. He called us "very stupid, brave girls."

Mum wasn't nearly as angry as I thought she'd be. She was cross that we'd been following again (even though I explained that we weren't, we were just watching), but I think she was pleased that Rajinder had found out who had been putting the leaflets through the door.

And when Mrs Blake came round to complain about me, Mum told her if she ever laid a hand on me again, she'd report her to the police.

All summer, the boycott grew. People told people, who told other people, who told more people, until it seemed as if everyone on the estate knew about it.

And now the summer was nearly over, and Rajinder and I were standing together outside the boarded-up shop.

"Where do you think he's gone?" I asked Rajinder.

"I don't know and I don't care. As far away from here as possible, I hope. Horrible man," she said.

We stood there for a while, both of us wrapped up in our own thoughts. Finally, Rajinder broke the silence.

"Come on," she said. "Let's go and tell everyone."

We started to walk away, but I turned round once more, just to make sure.

It had been hard work getting all those people to join in.

But it had been worth it. The boycott had worked.

Carter's Newsagent
Premises to Rent